INTERESTING FACTS ABOUT PHILIPPINES

BEAUTIFUL PHOTOGRAPHY PHOTOBOOK FROM PHILIPPINES WITH TRAVEL FACTS FOR CHILDREN

Copyright @2023 James K. Mahi

TABLE OF CONTENT

What is the national animal of the Philippines?

The national animal of the Philippines is the Carabao (water buffalo).

What is the national tree of the Denmark ?

The beech tree (Fagus sylvatica) is considered the national tree of Denmark.

What is the national sport of the Philippines?

The national sport of the Philippines is Arnis, a traditional Filipino martial art.

What is the national tree of the Philippines?

The national tree of the Philippines is the Narra (Pterocarpus indicus).

What is the official name of the Philippines?

The official name of the Philippines is the Republic of the Philippines.

What are the people of the Philippines called?

The people of the Philippines are called Filipinos.

How big is the Philippines?

The Philippines has a total land area of approximately 300,000 square kilometers (115,831 square miles).

What percentage of the world's land does the Philippines occupy?

The Philippines occupies less than 0.1% of the world's land area.

What is the population of the Philippines?

The population of the Philippines is approximately 113 million people.

Is the Philippines overly populated?

The Philippines has a relatively high population density, especially in urban areas. Some regions may be considered densely populated, while others are more sparsely populated.

How many provinces does the Philippines have?

The Philippines is divided into 81 provinces.

What percentage of the Philippines is covered by rainforests?

Approximately 20% of the Philippines is covered by rainforests.

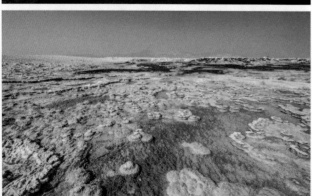

What is the Philippines' nickname?

The Philippines is often referred to as the "Pearl of the Orient Seas" or simply the "Pearl of the Orient."

What was the old name of the Philippines?

The Philippines was named after King Philip II of Spain and was previously known as the Spanish East Indies or Las Islas Filipinas.

Which months are the coldest in the Philippines?

The coldest months in the Philippines are typically from December to February.

Which months are the hottest in the Philippines?

The hottest months in the Philippines are typically from April to May.

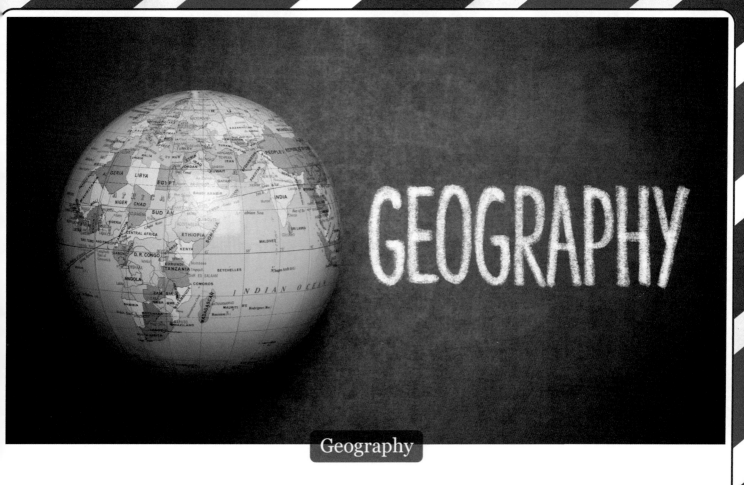

Geography

- The Philippines is an archipelago consisting of 7,641 islands, making it the second-largest archipelago in the world.
- Mount Apo, located in Mindanao, is the highest peak in the Philippines, standing at an elevation of 9,692 feet (2,954 meters).
- The country is home to the Chocolate Hills, a unique geological formation consisting of over 1,200 perfectly cone-shaped hills located in Bohol.
- The Tubbataha Reefs Natural Park in Palawan is a UNESCO World Heritage Site and is considered one of the best diving spots in the world.
- The Philippines lies on the Pacific Ring of Fire, resulting in frequent earthquakes and volcanic activity. It is home to over 20 active volcanoes.

History

- The Philippines was colonized by Spain for more than 300 years until it gained independence on June 12, 1898.
- The country was occupied by Japan during World War II from 1942 to 1945, resulting in significant destruction and loss of life.
- Ferdinand Marcos ruled the Philippines as a dictator from 1965 to 1986, leading to widespread corruption and human rights abuses.
- The People Power Revolution in 1986 was a nonviolent uprising that overthrew Marcos and restored democracy in the Philippines.
- The Philippines was a former U.S. colony and gained full independence on July 4, 1946.

Sports

- Basketball is the most popular sport in the Philippines, and it is often referred to as the country's national sport.
- Manny Pacquiao, a Filipino professional boxer, is considered one of the greatest boxers of all time and has won numerous world titles in multiple weight divisions.
- Arnis, a Filipino martial art, is the national sport and martial art of the Philippines.
- Football (soccer) is also gaining popularity in the country, and the Philippine national football team, known as the Azkals, has been improving in international competitions.
- Traditional Filipino games, such as sipa (kick volleyball) and luksong tinik (jumping over thorns), are still played in local communities.

Animals

- The Philippine eagle, also known as the monkey-eating eagle, is one of the world's largest and rarest eagle species, found only in the Philippines.
- Tarsiers, small primates with large round eyes, are endemic to the Philippines and are considered one of the world's smallest primates.
- The dugong, also known as the sea cow, can be found in the waters surrounding the Philippines. It is a herbivorous marine mammal.
- The Philippine tarsier and the tamaraw (a dwarf buffalo) are both listed as critically endangered species.
- The Philippines is home to a wide variety of colorful and unique marine life, making it a popular destination for diving and snorkeling.

Government

- The Philippines is a democratic republic with a presidential form of government.
- The President of the Philippines serves as both the head of state and the head of government.
- The country has a bicameral legislature, consisting of the Senate and the House of Representatives.
- The current constitution of the Philippines, known as the 1987 Constitution, was ratified after the fall of the Marcos dictatorship.
- The Philippines follows a multi-party system, with political parties playing a crucial role in the country's elections.

Economy

- The Philippines has a developing mixed economy with agriculture, manufacturing, and services sectors contributing to its GDP.
- The country is one of the world's largest exporters of electronic products, including semiconductors and electronic components.
- The business process outsourcing (BPO) industry is a significant contributor to the Philippine economy, providing services such as call centers, data entry, and software development.
- Remittances from overseas Filipino workers (OFWs) play a crucial role in the economy, with billions of dollars being sent back to the country each year.
- Tourism is also a vital sector for the Philippine economy, attracting millions of visitors annually with its beautiful beaches, cultural heritage, and natural wonders.

Currency

- The currency of the Philippines is the Philippine Peso (PHP), which is further divided into centavos.
- Banknotes in circulation include denominations of 20, 50, 100, 200, 500, and 1,000 pesos, while coins come in denominations of 1, 5, and 10 pesos, as well as smaller centavo coins.
- The Bangko Sentral ng Pilipinas (Central Bank of the Philippines) is responsible for issuing and regulating the country's currency.
- The Philippine Peso symbol is ₱, which represents the currency in financial transactions and displays.
- When traveling to the Philippines, it's advisable to exchange currency at authorized banks or exchange centers for better rates and security.

Import and Exports

- The Philippines exports various goods, including electronics, garments, coconut oil, machinery, and mineral products.
- Major export destinations for Philippine products include the United States, Japan, China, Hong Kong, and Singapore.
- In terms of imports, the Philippines primarily purchases electronic products, mineral fuels, machinery, transport equipment, and iron and steel.
- Key import partners for the country include China, Japan, South Korea, the United States, and Thailand.
- The Philippines participates in international trade through memberships in organizations such as the World Trade Organization (WTO) and the Association of Southeast Asian Nations (ASEAN).

Culture

- Filipino culture is a vibrant blend of indigenous, Malay, Spanish, and American influences due to the country's history of colonization and cultural exchange.
- The Philippines is known for its traditional arts and crafts, such as weaving, pottery, wood carving, and metalwork.
- Filipino cuisine reflects the country's diverse heritage, with dishes like adobo (marinated meat), sinigang (sour soup), and lechon (roast pig) being popular favorites.
- Festivals are an integral part of Filipino culture, with colorful celebrations happening throughout the year, such as the Sinulog Festival in Cebu and the Ati-Atihan Festival in Kalibo.
- Bayanihan, a Filipino custom of communal unity and cooperation, is deeply rooted in the culture, promoting the value of helping one another and working together as a community.

People

- Filipinos are known for their hospitality and friendliness, often referred to as one of the warmest and most welcoming cultures in the world.
- The Philippines has a population of over 110 million people, making it the 13th most populous country globally.
- Tagalog, also known as Filipino, is the national language, but there are over 170 different languages and dialects spoken throughout the country.
- The Filipino diaspora is significant, with a large number of Filipinos living and working abroad, particularly in the United States, Saudi Arabia, the United Arab Emirates, and Canada.
- The literacy rate in the Philippines is relatively high, with education being highly valued and accessible to the majority of the population.

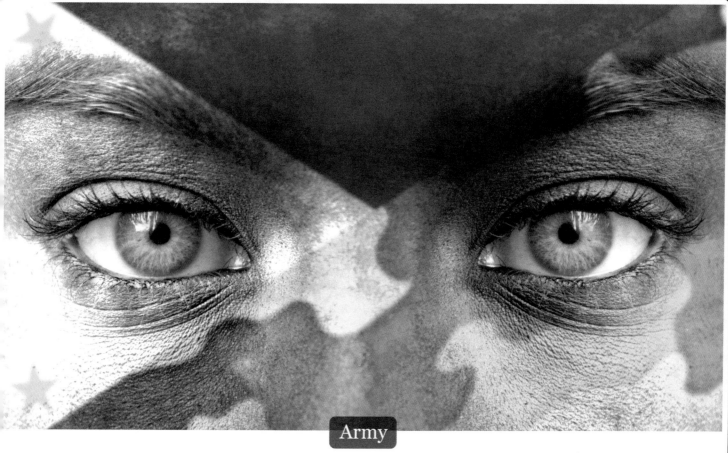

Army

- The Armed Forces of the Philippines (AFP) is the military organization responsible for the defense and security of the country.
- It consists of three main branches: the Philippine Army, the Philippine Navy, and the Philippine Air Force.
- The AFP has a long history of involvement in both domestic and international peacekeeping missions, providing support and assistance in conflict-affected areas.
- The Philippine Army is the largest branch of the AFP and plays a crucial role in maintaining peace and stability within the country.
- The AFP also conducts joint military exercises and collaborations with allied nations, including the United States and other Southeast Asian countries, to enhance its capabilities and promote regional security.

Tourism

- The Philippines is known for its stunning natural landscapes, attracting tourists from around the world. Popular destinations include the world-renowned beaches of Boracay, Palawan, and Siargao.
- The country boasts diverse marine biodiversity, making it a top destination for diving and snorkeling enthusiasts.
- Historical sites like the walled city of Intramuros in Manila and the UNESCO World Heritage-listed town of Vigan showcase the country's rich cultural heritage.
- Adventure seekers can enjoy activities such as trekking to the crater of Mount Pinatubo or exploring the underground river in Puerto Princesa.
- The Philippines is also famous for its festivals, such as the Ati-Atihan Festival, Panagbenga Festival, and Pahiyas Festival, which showcase vibrant costumes, dances, and traditional music.

VISA APPLICATION

Visas

- Foreign visitors to the Philippines typically require a visa unless they come from visa-exempt countries. Nationals of some countries are allowed visa-free entry for a limited period.
- The Philippine government offers various types of visas, including tourist visas, business visas, and work visas, depending on the purpose and duration of stay.
- Tourist visas are usually granted for stays of 30 days but can be extended for up to 59 days.
- Longer-term visas, such as work visas, require sponsorship from a local employer or company and must comply with specific requirements set by the Bureau of Immigration.
- It's essential for travelers to check the specific visa requirements and regulations before planning their visit to the Philippines.

Food

- Filipino cuisine is a delightful fusion of flavors influenced by Spanish, Chinese, Malay, and American cooking traditions.
- Popular Filipino dishes include adobo (a savory meat stew), sinigang (a sour soup), lechon (roast pig), and pancit (noodles).
- Rice is a staple food in the Philippines, and it is often served with every meal.
- Street food culture is vibrant in the Philippines, offering a wide array of snacks and delicacies like balut (boiled duck embryo), isaw (grilled chicken intestines), and halo-halo (a refreshing dessert).
- The Philippines is also known for its sweet treats, including bibingka (rice cake), leche flan (caramel custard), and ube halaya (purple yam jam).

Language

- Filipino and English are the official languages of the Philippines.
- Filipino, based on Tagalog, is the national language and serves as a lingua franca among Filipinos from different regions.
- English is widely spoken and used in schools, government, business, and the media. It plays a vital role in communication and is considered a significant advantage in the job market.
- There are also numerous regional languages and dialects spoken across the country, reflecting the rich linguistic diversity of the Philippines.
- The ability to speak English has made the Philippines a popular destination for outsourcing services, such as call centers and business process outsourcing.

Religion

- The Philippines is predominantly Christian, with Catholicism being the largest religious affiliation. The country has the third-largest Catholic population in the world.
- Other significant Christian denominations include Protestantism and various independent Christian groups.
- Islam is the second-largest religion in the Philippines, particularly concentrated in the southern region of Mindanao.
- There are also smaller communities practicing Buddhism, Hinduism, and indigenous animistic beliefs.
- Religious festivals and traditions hold immense cultural importance in the Philippines, with colorful processions, fiestas, and religious rites celebrated throughout the year.

Holidays

- The Philippines celebrates a variety of national and regional holidays throughout the year.
- Christmas season, known as "Pasko," is widely celebrated and is one of the longest and most festive holiday periods in the country. It usually begins in September and lasts until early January.
- Holy Week, particularly Good Friday, is a significant religious observance marked by processions and reenactments of the crucifixion of Jesus Christ in some areas of the country.
- Independence Day, celebrated on June 12th, commemorates the country's declaration of independence from Spain in 1898.
- Other holidays include New Year's Day, Labor Day, All Saints' Day, and Rizal Day, which honors the national hero, Jose Rizal.

Cost of Living

- The cost of living in the Philippines can vary significantly depending on the region and city.
- In general, living expenses in rural areas and smaller cities tend to be lower compared to major metropolitan areas like Manila and Cebu.
- Housing costs, such as rent or property prices, can vary greatly depending on the location and type of accommodation.
- Food and groceries are relatively affordable, especially when purchasing local produce and products.
- Transportation costs, including public transportation fares and fuel prices, are generally reasonable, although traffic congestion can be a challenge in urban areas.

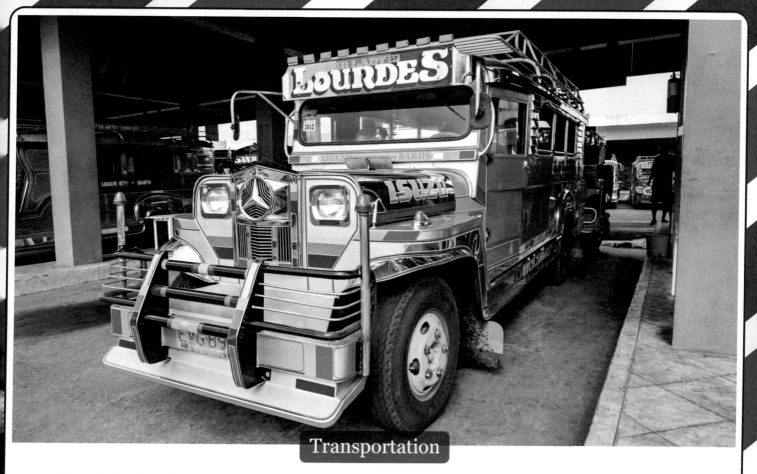

Transportation

- The Philippines has a variety of transportation options, including jeepneys (colorful and modified jeeps), tricycles (motorcycles with sidecars), and buses, which are commonly used for short-distance travel within cities and towns.
- Taxis and ride-hailing services like Grab are available in urban areas and can be more convenient for longer journeys.
- Domestic air travel is popular for traveling between different islands, with several local airlines offering flights to various destinations.
- The country has an extensive network of ferries, particularly in areas with numerous islands, providing transportation for both passengers and goods.
- Traffic congestion can be an issue in major cities, so it's advisable to plan travel accordingly and consider alternate transportation options such as the metro rail systems in Manila and Cebu.

Relationship with Other Countries

- The Philippines maintains diplomatic relations with numerous countries around the world.
- As a member of the Association of Southeast Asian Nations (ASEAN), the Philippines actively participates in regional cooperation and dialogue.
- The United States has historically been a close ally and important economic partner of the Philippines, with shared military cooperation and cultural ties.
- The Philippines also maintains strong ties with other countries, including Japan, China, Australia, South Korea, and countries in the European Union.
- The country actively engages in international organizations such as the United Nations (UN), the World Trade Organization (WTO), and the Asia-Pacific Economic Cooperation (APEC).

Time Zone

- The Philippines Standard Time (PST) is UTC+8 and does not observe daylight saving time.
- The country operates on a single time zone throughout its islands, making it more convenient for travel and communication within the country.
- PST is 8 hours ahead of Coordinated Universal Time (UTC), which serves as the global time standard.
- It's important to consider the time difference when scheduling international communication or travel arrangements with other countries.
- Some neighboring countries, such as China, share the same time zone as the Philippines, facilitating business and diplomatic interactions.

Healthcare

- The Philippines has a mixed healthcare system consisting of both public and private healthcare facilities.
- The government provides healthcare services through the Philippine Health Insurance Corporation (PhilHealth) to eligible citizens and permanent residents.
- Private healthcare facilities, including hospitals and clinics, offer a wide range of medical services, and many have modern facilities and highly trained medical professionals.
- Access to healthcare can vary across regions, with more remote areas often having limited medical facilities and resources.
- It's advisable for travelers to have comprehensive travel insurance that covers medical expenses when visiting the Philippines.

Education

- Education is highly valued in the Philippines, with a compulsory and free public education system for elementary and high school levels.
- The country has a literacy rate of over 95%, indicating a high level of educational attainment among its population.
- Higher education institutions, including universities and colleges, offer a wide range of academic programs and professional courses.
- English is the primary medium of instruction in schools, making the Philippines a popular destination for international students seeking quality education in an English-speaking environment.
- The country has produced a significant number of skilled professionals, including doctors, nurses, engineers, and IT specialists, who are sought after in both local and international job markets.

Crime and Safety

- Like any other country, the Philippines has areas with higher crime rates, particularly in urban centers. It's advisable for travelers to exercise caution and be aware of their surroundings, especially in unfamiliar areas.
- It's recommended to take precautions such as keeping valuables secure, avoiding displaying expensive items, and being vigilant in crowded places.
- The Philippine government and local law enforcement agencies continuously work to improve public safety and maintain peace and order.
- Some tourist destinations, particularly in popular beach and resort areas, have dedicated tourist police units to ensure the safety of visitors.
- It's always a good idea to stay informed about current safety advisories and follow the guidance of local authorities and travel advisories issued by your home country's embassy or consulate.

Top 10 Travel Places in Philippines

Boracay – Known for its white sand beaches and vibrant nightlife.

Palawan - Home to stunning limestone cliffs, crystal-clear waters, and the famous Underground River in Puerto Princesa.

Siargao - A paradise for surfers, with world-class waves and a laid-back island vibe.

Banaue Rice Terraces – Ancient rice terraces carved into the mountainside, showcasing the ingenuity of the indigenous Ifugao people.

Cebu – A bustling city with historical landmarks, vibrant festivals, and nearby diving spots.

Bohol – Famous for its Chocolate Hills, tarsiers (one of the world's smallest primates), and beautiful beaches.

Vigan - A UNESCO World Heritage Site, known for its well-preserved Spanish colonial architecture.

Davao - Located in Mindanao, it offers a mix of urban attractions, natural wonders, and the iconic Mount Apo, the highest peak in the Philippines.

Sagada - A scenic mountain town known for its hanging coffins, caves, waterfalls, and breathtaking views.

Batanes - A remote group of islands known for its dramatic landscapes, rolling hills, and picturesque lighthouses.

Made in the USA
Las Vegas, NV
07 December 2023

82285947R00026